ELLEN SWIFT

ROMAN DRESS
ACCESSORIES

SHIRE ARCHAEOLOGY

2

Cover illustration:
Romano-British dragonesque brooch. (© The British Museum)

British Library Cataloguing in Publication Data:
Swift, Ellen.
Roman Dress Accessories. – (Shire archaeology; 85)
1. Costume jewelry – Great Britain – History – To 1500
2. Jewelry, Classical – Great Britain
3. Dress Accessories – Great Britain – History – To 1500
4. Dress accessories – Rome – History – To 1500
5. Costume – Great Britain – History – To 1500
6. Costume – Rome – History – To 1500
7. Great Britain – Antiquities, Roman
I. Title 391.7'09361
ISBN 0 7478 0567 9

Published in 2003 by
SHIRE PUBLICATIONS LTD
Cromwell House, Church Street, Princes Risborough,
Buckinghamshire HP27 9AA, UK.
(Website: www.shirebooks.co.uk)

Series Editor: James Dyer.

Number 85 in the Shire Archaeology series.

ISBN 0 7478 0567 9.

First published 2003.

Printed in Malta by
Gutenberg Press Limited, Gudja Road, Tarxien PLA 19, Malta

Contents

Acknowledgements

Thanks are due to Guy de la Bédoyère, Alex Croom, Richard Hobbs, Michael Lewis, and the museums and other organisations that assisted with the illustrations and permission to reproduce images, and to Hester Swift who kindly proof-read the text.

List of illustrations

1
Introduction

This book is about dress accessories rather than jewellery. When Roman archaeologists and jewellery historians write about Roman 'jewellery', they usually use the term to mean objects made from gold, silver and precious stones. Items in these materials have always been perceived as valuable and form a significant part of many museum collections. They have been studied primarily in terms of either aesthetics or the techniques of the goldsmith. It can be difficult, though, to move beyond this kind of analysis to consider the use and significance of particular items of precious metal jewellery. Gold and silver objects are not often accompanied by surviving details of where they were found or on what kind of site; frequently they are items that have been bought or donated to museums by private collectors and we no longer know where they were made or how they were used. We may not even know how old they are, though artefacts can often be given an approximate date range on stylistic grounds. There is an added problem that, because of the intrinsic value of gold and precious materials, many precious metal objects would not have been found in a context bearing any relation to their original use anyway; gold jewellery, for example, is often buried in hoards, in which its economic value supersedes its original function.

Since the early twentieth century, however, large quantities of more prosaic items from everyday life have been recovered from archaeological excavations and deposited in museums, and, bringing excavated material into play, it is possible to put a greater focus on 'jewellery' in other materials, such as copper alloy, bone and glass. These objects are often termed simply 'small finds' in archaeological reports, or they may be called 'personal ornaments' or 'dress accessories' to distinguish them from the élite connotations of the word 'jewellery' and to include items that we would not automatically think of as jewellery, such as belt fittings or shoe buckles.

These objects have much more to tell us about the ordinary person and life in Roman Britain or the Roman Empire than a unique piece of gold jewellery. Where they come from excavated contexts we are in a much better position to investigate their use within a particular society or culture. This book therefore provides an introduction to non-precious metal items – dress accessories – rather than jewellery, and how these can be identified and used by archaeologists in their study of the past.

The adoption of Roman-style dress

In the pre-Roman period, jewellery and dress accessories were worn, and we might particularly associate the Iron Age period with items such as gold torcs (neck rings of penannular form made from cables of twisted wire). Such torcs are worn by 'barbarians' on some sculptures from the Roman period, and we can surmise that they became a useful way to symbolise the indigenous population in some areas of the Roman Empire, whether or not they were worn widely as part of local dress. In some Roman provinces, the local people continued to wear the 'traditional' dress that had been worn before the Roman conquest; for example, in areas of the Roman province of *Noricum* (modern-day Austria), women carried on their custom of wearing brooches in pairs to pin the tunic until the second century AD (Garbsch 1965: 32). As provinces became subject to Roman authority, new, 'Roman-style' items of dress also became popular. These were not worn only by the Roman élite, but were widely adopted by local populations under Roman rule, becoming more and more common through time as indigenous traditions gradually diminished. Bracelets and rings, for example, were not common in Britain before the Roman occupation (Johns 1996: 108), but precious metal examples of bracelets and some made from copper alloy and other materials are known from the early Roman period. Non-precious metal bracelets show a burgeoning popularity in the later Roman period, particularly the fourth century. Glass beads were worn before the Roman conquest but these were very different in appearance to Roman-style beads (Guido 1978), which became gradually more popular through the centuries of Roman occupation in the different provinces. By the fourth century AD, a distinctive provincial Roman culture had developed in each province with the widespread use of 'Roman-style' dress accessories among all sectors of the population.

Using evidence from studies carried out in the late twentieth century, the following chapters will examine this provincial Roman culture, looking at production areas, distribution patterns and the locations of workshops, and giving an overview of brooches, bracelets, beads, necklaces, rings, earrings, pins, and belt sets. Frequently occurring types and styles will be described, enabling the reader to identify objects commonly found in museums and on archaeological sites. Chapters on the different types of dress accessories worn in the Roman period will be followed by a discussion of the wider study of dress accessories and what it can tell us about the past.

2
Production systems and distribution

The technology to produce dress accessories from materials such as glass, bone and metal is relatively straightforward and requires no special skills or sophisticated equipment. In turn, most of the raw materials themselves are available universally. It is therefore not surprising that items such as pins, rings and brooches were produced in many different workshops scattered throughout the Empire. In general, we might assume that most items were produced and distributed fairly locally, to meet consumer demand in each area, and this is borne out by the existence of many regional types and styles of brooch, bracelet and so on with quite limited distribution (figure 1), though there are some exceptions, such

1. This map shows the distribution of four-strand cable bracelets with a particular kind of fastening, which is limited to a specific region in the Danube area. (© Ellen Swift)

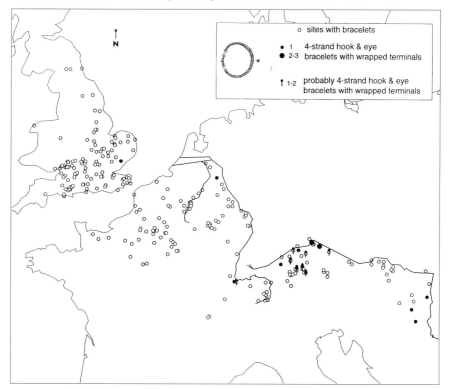

2. Tombstone or shrine of a smith at work. It is rare to find metalworking evidence from the Roman period, but we do have a number of depictions of metal smiths at work, such as this one from York. (© Guy de la Bédoyère)

as crossbow brooches (figure 11), many of which were produced in a large state-run production centre in the Roman province of *Pannonia*, modern-day Hungary (Swift 2000a: 88).

There is some variation in more unusual types of material available in each area of the Roman Empire. For example, jet, which was used to make pins and bracelets, occurs only in isolated spots in Britain and Germany. As we might expect, jet objects are much more common in the area surrounding Whitby in Yorkshire (where one can still find lumps of jet on the beach today) than they are elsewhere in the Empire. It is interesting to map the spread of jet objects further afield. Since the origin point for the raw material is known, the distribution pattern of jet objects will provide useful information about the trading

practices of workshops in the Roman period. It must be remembered, however, that, as jet was a relatively unusual material, the demand for jet objects in more remote areas may have prompted trade over wider distances than would be likely to occur for objects made of metal or glass.

Studying distribution patterns is an important way of looking at production and marketing systems, since it is rare to find concrete evidence for the existence of workshops, although metal smiths are sometimes depicted in Roman

3. Metalwork moulds from Alcester, Warwickshire. Moulds such as these are among the few sources of evidence for the production of metal objects in a particular area. (© R. Wilkins)

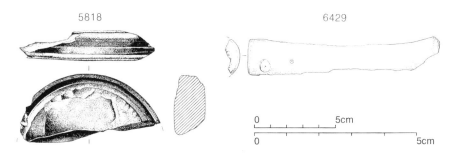

4. Jet and antler waste from 9 Blake Street, York, showing that craft activities were carried out in this area. (© York Archaeological Trust)

art (figure 2). Evidence for craftspeople working in metal might include crucibles and furnaces, jewellers' tools and equipment, partially finished objects, off-cuts, casts, moulds (figure 3) and scrap-metal collections. Workers in materials such as bone or ivory would leave behind turnings, tools, blanks and so on. For example, excavations at Blake Street in York yielded a jet 'waster' (Cool, Lloyd-Morgan and Hooley 1995: 1597) – a disc-shaped piece of jet left over from the manufacture of a bracelet (figure 4). A few notable sites exist with more extensive collections of objects and residue, indicating the definite presence of a workshop.

The glass-bead workshop at Trier

The Rhineland of Germany was the heartland of Roman glass production. Many different vessel types were produced in the region, and Trier (located midway between the Rhine and Luxembourg) and Cologne (Köln) were important centres. The importance of such towns in the Roman glass industry can easily be grasped by visiting the Römisch-Germanisch Museum at Cologne, which holds an extensive collection of Roman glass. At Trier, an excavation carried out in the early twentieth century provides the only known evidence from the Roman period for the existence of a workshop specifically for the production of beads. The remains of a crucible were found, together with off-cuts of glass and numerous annular opaque glass beads decorated with trailed patterns in different coloured glass (Swift 2000a: 115). These beads became very popular in the late fourth century and early fifth century in the Roman Empire. As we might expect from the presence of the workshop, many beads have been found at or near Trier, but they have also been found at numerous other sites widely scattered throughout the Empire and beyond.

The more common type of Roman glass bead is a small one-colour bead of translucent glass, probably made by cutting a pierced rod into lengths. It is surmised that one-colour beads were probably produced alongside vessel glass in less specialised workshops.

As Van der Sleen (1973) describes in a book about glass beads, the basic raw ingredients are sand, lime and soda or potash. These natural materials contain impurities such as iron and, as a result, the glass produced is naturally of a greenish-blue translucent colour (often called 'natural' glass). Natural glass was not much used for beads, and it would be converted into colourless or coloured glass. The green-blue colour could be removed by adding manganese or antimony. This was more difficult, though, than making coloured glass, which could be produced by adding chemicals such as copper or cobalt (which would make blue beads, for example).

In bead making, the crucible containing the raw materials would be heated to a very high temperature to produce molten glass. Simply piercing a drop of molten glass with a tool before it had solidified would be the easiest method of making a bead, but this would not give much control over the final shape. To produce greater regularity in the shape of the bead, an implement would be dipped in the liquid glass and pulled away to create a strand that would solidify into a rod of coloured glass. Beads could be produced from these rods in a number of different ways. A widely used method in the Roman period was to soften the canes of glass and wrap a section round a hot wire before cutting it off. The segmented beads made by this process can be easily identified. Another method of making a perforation through a bead is relatively sophisticated. Before the glass cane from which the bead is made was produced, an air-bubble would be worked into the molten glass. When a strand of glass was drawn out, care would be taken to include the air-bubble, which would be stretched out, forming a long, hollow rod when the strand of glass had solidified. To make the geometric shapes popular for Roman beads, a still malleable, cooling section of glass rod could be pushed into a mould of the desired shape.

The Roman temple at Lydney and the production of bronze dress accessories

In the Roman period, it was common for votive offerings of objects, inscriptions and so on to be deposited in the sacred spring at temple sites. The site at Lydney Park in Gloucestershire (figure 5 shows a possible reconstruction of the temple), which was excavated in the 1920s, produced a large collection of this material including over 270 copper alloy bracelets (figure 6). There is also some evidence for metalworking at Lydney and it has been suggested that the bracelets

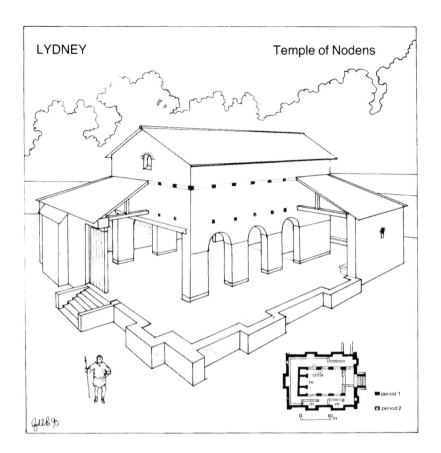

LYDNEY

Temple of Nodens

5. (Above) Reconstruction of the Temple of Nodens at Lydney Park, Gloucestershire. (© Guy de la Bédoyère)

6. (Right) Range of bracelets found at Lydney Park, including examples with cut and notched decoration, punched circle and dot decoration and multiple-motif decoration. Over 270 bracelets, thought to be a votive offering, were found at the site; those published by Wheeler in his excavation report are only a fraction of the total number, which are in private ownership. (After Wheeler and Wheeler 1932)

were produced on-site.

Bracelets could be produced in a number of different ways. The most time-consuming would be to make cast bracelets from moulds into which the molten metal could be poured. These do exist in the Roman period, but their numbers are far outweighed by bracelets produced in simpler ways. Perhaps the most popular method, known also in the pre-Roman Iron Age, was to take several strands of wire and to twist these around one another to form a cable, which could be bent into a circular shape. One strand of wire would be twisted into a hook and eye at either end. A variation on this technique would be to use just one strand of wire with a square section. Twisting this would result in a spiral pattern running around the wire, formed by the edges of the cube. This was a popular bracelet type in Britain. Twisted bracelets, or just single strands of round-sectioned wire, might be fastened around the wrist by using overlapping sections of wire, held by loops, which could be slid over one another to decrease the size of the bracelet so that it would not fall over the hand. Decorated bracelets were very common in the late Roman period especially, and these would often be made from lengths of sheet bronze, cut to size and stamped with patterns. Similar techniques using cast bronze and wire and sheet metal would have been used to make other metal jewellery; some more detailed examples of decorative styles used on particular items are given later in this book.

The Snettisham Roman jeweller's hoard

A discovery made near the site of a famous Iron Age treasure hoard, the Snettisham Roman jeweller's hoard, is the best example so far discovered of a collection of jeweller's material (Johns 1997). It includes finished and unfinished objects, tools and scrap metal. Though it seems that this particular workshop produced high-status jewellery only, it is still an invaluable find for our knowledge of workshops in general. The finds even provide some evidence concerning the numbers of people employed in specific tasks in this particular workshop. A large number of intaglios were discovered. These are carved gemstones usually set into rings, often depicting Roman gods and mythical figures (figure 7). An extremely detailed examination of the carving techniques revealed that each specialist craftsperson had his or her own style of engraving. From this, it was deduced that three craftspeople worked as engravers in the Snettisham workshop.

One of the most interesting finds at Snettisham was the collection of silver coins assembled by the craftspeople. It was found that the workers had deliberately selected coins with a high silver content, from the years before the coinage became excessively debased. These coins would presumably have been melted down and used to manufacture objects.

7. Intaglio of Victory. Such carved gemstones, usually set into rings, carried motifs of gods, goddesses and other popular themes, such as animals, which might also have a particular association with a specific deity. Details of the carving technique sometimes enable the archaeologist to identify an intaglio as the product of a particular workshop or even an individual craftsman. (© Guy de la Bédoyère)

Production of bone, jet, shale and wooden dress accessories

Since wooden objects do not survive well in the archaeological record, we can only guess at how popular this material was for the manufacture of dress accessories. Other materials such as bone are also more fragile than copper alloy but survive relatively well under some soil conditions. The property that these raw materials share, though, is their inability to be melted and cast as glass and metal can be, and they therefore require quite different manufacturing techniques. Since they do not need the high temperatures necessary to manipulate glass and metal, production need not be confined to workshops, and many objects may have been made by individuals for their personal use. Techniques of manufacture might include carving, or sawing the raw material into flat sections and working these by hand, or with the assistance of a lathe (this process being known as 'turning').

Most of the common dress accessories in the Roman period discussed in the following chapters were produced in the full range of materials – copper alloy, glass, bone, jet, shale, ivory – though some raw materials undoubtedly lend themselves more readily to one object type than another.

3
Brooches

When excavating a Roman site, or perhaps walking a field in which scatterings of Roman pottery, brick and tile are evident, the Roman dress accessory that you are most likely to find is a brooch. Brooches were certainly popular items of dress in the Roman period and there is a wide variety of different types. The other reason why brooches are frequent finds, however, is probably because they are fairly recognisable and substantial items. Bracelets, rings and earrings are thin, easily broken, easily missed and prone to a very general interpretation, for example as a 'ring' – which could come from any kind of attachment – rather than, necessarily, a 'finger-ring' or whatever (especially if they are somewhat corroded). This is particularly likely to happen in the case of earrings, which may be very small and fragmentary, or misleadingly similar to other types of ring attachments (see Allason-Jones 1989).

Brooches, however, are rather more recognisable, and also better studied, perhaps a direct result of the larger numbers that have been found. One of the most widely known Romano-British artefacts is the so-called 'dragonesque' brooch – a beautiful, sinuous, enamelled creation, elegantly portraying a very stylised double-headed animal (see the cover of this book). There are also many other different types of brooch that were worn in the Roman period; some of the most common types are discussed below and illustrated in figure 8. A number of publications have brought together useful collections of material that can be used as a reference guide for particular variants of each type; some are listed in the bibliography at the end of this book.

Bow brooches

The most obvious function for a brooch is to fasten two pieces of clothing together, and in a time before clothes fasteners were attached to an item of clothing itself, it is easy to see how important brooches must have been. Bow brooches, with their very functional appearance, are a good illustration of this – they seem to be there simply to carry out a particular task. In its most rudimentary form a bow brooch might consist of a folded wire held by a catch at the base. By making one or two coils in the wire, creating some tension, the difficulty of pressing the pin back into the catch can be increased, making it less likely that the brooch will accidentally come unfastened. If the loop of the wire (called the bow) is made bigger, it will be possible to contain a larger piece of cloth, or several thicker layers of fabric. For ease of fastening, the simple sprung-pin mechanism might be replaced by a hinged pin. In

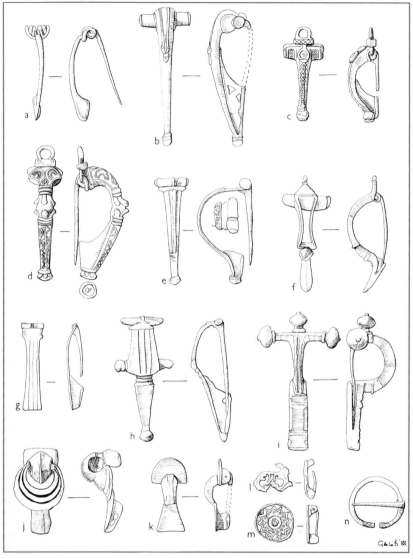

8. Roman brooch types: (a) Nauheim-derivative; (b) Polden Hill; (c) head-stud; (d) trumpet; (e) Aucissa; (f) divided bow; (g) Langton Down; (h) Hod Hill; (i) crossbow; (j) thistle; (k) knee; (l) enamelled plate; (m) enamelled disc; (n) penannular. (© Guy de la Bédoyère)

this way we can see how the bow brooch developed and how its form is intimately linked to function. The beauty of a purely functional object cannot be disputed, and some of the most simple bow brooches are also to some eyes the most appealing. However, the wide range of bow brooches found in the Roman period in Britain and other provinces also includes many types that have additional decorative features. Some of the more common types of bow brooch are described below.

Nauheim-derivatives

This type of brooch was known before the Roman conquest and continued to be used in the first century AD. It is very simple, consisting of a wire wound to form a sprung pin held by a catch plate (figure 8, a).

Aucissa brooches

This brooch type takes its name from the stamped letters 'Aucissa' sometimes found on the head. It is thought that the type was made in Gaul in the first century AD. It has a flat decorated bow, rolled up at the head end to hold the hinged pin (figure 8, e). Variants of this brooch type exist, such as Colchester brooches with a less decorated bow, and Hod Hill brooches, which are frequently decorated with ribbing. Colchester and Hod Hill brooches were probably made in Britain.

Trumpet brooches

These often highly decorated brooches were current in the late first and early second century in Britain and are a Romano-British type (Johns 1996). They rather resemble a miniature harp when viewed from the side, with a strongly curving bow widening out at the head (hence the 'trumpet' name) to conceal the spring or hinge of the pin behind (figures 8d and 9). The decoration may be cast, engraved or enamelled.

Crossbow brooches

A late Roman type, dating from the very end of the third century to the mid-to-late fifth century AD, and particularly popular in the middle years of the fourth century, this type of brooch has a bow balanced by a cross-piece and an extended foot (figure 10). In its most characteristic form the brooch has three large onion-shaped knobs on the terminals of the bow and cross-piece. The pin is hinged. The crossbow brooch is particularly associated with the military and with high-status civilians. Some carry inscriptions with the emperor's name, chi-rho motifs (a common early Christian symbol) or portrait medallions, thought to be of the emperor. Very late crossbow brooches have one particularly unusual feature rarely found in antiquity – a screw mechanism. The knobs on the ends of the

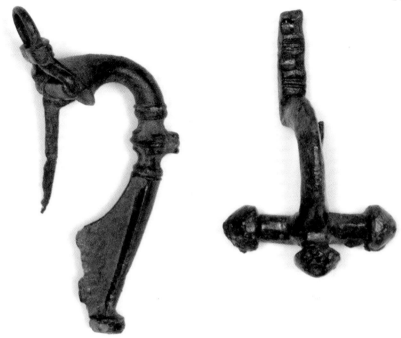

9. (Above left) Trumpet brooch. The expanding upper part of the bow resembles a trumpet bell. (© Tyne & Wear Museums)

10. (Above right) Crossbow brooch. Brooches of this type are known to have been used as symbols of high status among both the military and civilians and were worn to pin the cloak on the right shoulder. There are many art-historical representations from the fourth century and later that show them being worn by men who held official positions in the late Roman world. (© Tyne & Wear Museums)

11. (Right) Crossbow brooch. This is one of the types of crossbow brooches that occur in large numbers in the Danube region; it was probably made in a state-run production centre in that area. (After Keller 1971)

cross-piece can be removed and are attached by means of a screw thread.

Plate brooches

As the name suggests, these were made from a flat piece of metal and invariably carry enamelled decoration, though some variants with glass settings or with repoussé decoration (patterns in relief made by applying pressure to the underside) are also known. They are found in a wide variety of shapes and the enamelled types date to the second century

12. Circular plate brooch, hare brooch and horse and rider brooch; these plate brooches are usually decorated with brightly coloured enamel, which does not always survive intact. (© Tyne & Wear Museums)

(Crummy 1983: 17). As well as geometric motifs such as circular and lozenge shapes, some brooches mimic different objects (skeumorphic) and animals (zoomorphic). Some examples are shown in figure 12.

Zoomorphic
This type of plate brooch is in the shape of an animal, decorated with brightly coloured enamel. Popular choices are hares, hounds, horses, horse and rider, cockerels and so on. Many of these animals are thought to have had symbolic significance in the Roman period, and some were linked to particular gods and goddesses; for example, the cockerel was associated with the god Mercury (Crummy 1983: 12). Some birds are represented in a more three-dimensional style, for example duck brooches with protuberant heads and plumage formed from crescent-shaped sections of coloured enamel.

Skeumorphic
This name is given to brooches that resemble something else. By far the most frequently occurring is a shoe brooch (the flat brooch mimics the appearance of the shoe sole) ornamented with enamel.

Dragonesque
These could be included in the zoomorphic category but are something

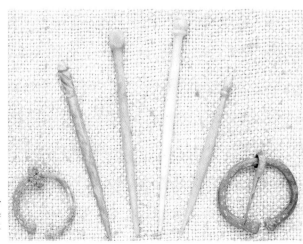

of a special case as they clearly do not depict a real animal, but rather one with two heads asymmetrically opposed to one another as if the creature is looking at its reflection in a pond (see cover photograph). The creature has a large ear and curled snout and the pin of the brooch is attached around its neck like a collar. This brooch type is Romano-British and clearly owes much to 'Celtic' art style, in which stylised rather than representational forms were preferred. Again, the brooch is most often enamelled. It is found in the first and early second centuries AD.

Glass set

This type of brooch is found in the first century and consists of a round or oval gilded disc with punched decoration and a central setting containing a glass 'gem' (figure 13). It is not found in very great numbers in Britain.

Penannular brooches

Penannular brooches are made from a simple open ring of metal with a pin looped around the ring. The pin is aligned with the gap in the ring and the ring can then be swivelled around to fasten the brooch. Such brooches are from the very early and very late Roman periods; examples found in York are shown in figure 14. They are also found from the first

14. Pins and penannular brooches from 9 Blake Street, York. (© York Archaeological Trust)

century BC and can therefore be regarded initially as the survival of an Iron Age or 'Celtic' tradition. Their reappearance in the fourth century has sometimes been regarded as part of a wider trend: the reappearance of 'Celtic' art styles. There are small differences between the early and late brooches, which enable the archaeologist to distinguish between them. Early brooches have solid terminal knobs whereas later penannulars have terminals that are flattened and then coiled up at right angles to the plane of the ring. Given the two-century gap between the different types, there is, however, some debate over whether they should be seen as part of the same tradition (see, for example, Fowler in Crummy 1983: 19).

Brooch distributions in Roman Britain

In an examination of the spread of brooches throughout Roman Britain, two things are immediately noticeable. First, some brooches have a distribution that is confined to a small geographic area and were seemingly worn only in that area. They were either made locally or imported from the Continent into a particular area. Generally, bow brooches, plate brooches and penannular brooches are found all over Roman Britain, but specific types of bow or plate brooch might be found in only one area. An example might be the bow brooch that is classified as Almgren's 'strongly profiled' type (a translation of the

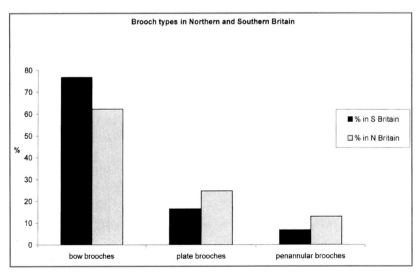

15. Brooch types in northern and southern Britain. Plate brooches and penannulars were apparently more popular in the north. (© Ellen Swift, from data by M. Snape)

German name), which has a distribution centring on London and Richborough and was apparently brought in by the military in the first century AD (Crummy 1983: 10). Second, there is a noticeable difference, pointed out by Margaret Snape (1993) in a corpus of Roman brooches from northern Britain, in the proportions of bow, plate and penannular brooches found in the north and the south (which can be roughly equated to military and non-military zones). She compared the brooches in her collection with R. Hattatt's compilation of brooches, which are mostly from southern Britain (Hattatt 1982, 1985, 1987). The results can be illustrated by means of a bar graph (figure 15). It can be seen that although there are roughly the same proportions of brooches relative to one another, plate and penannular brooches are more popular in the north than they are in the south. Snape also draws attention to the fact that the northern sample contains many more knee brooches (with an angled bow resembling a bent knee), P-brooches and crossbow brooches. This is consistent with the general opinion that P- and crossbow brooches at least were worn mostly by the military.

Brooch typology

The same type of brooch may be worn for many years, but in that time its appearance tends gradually to change, so that we can separate out brooches produced at different times. How types change over time can be best demonstrated by looking at the crossbow brooch, which developed out of the P-brooch in the late third to early fourth century and which was extremely common on military sites for much of the fourth century, continuing to be worn in the fifth century.

When this brooch first appears it looks very practical (a polite way of saying that it is rather unattractive to the modern eye), solid cast from copper alloy, with a large curving bow at the front to gather in the folds of cloth of a heavy military cloak. During the fourth and early fifth centuries it undergoes a dramatic transformation (figure 16). At first the brooch becomes slightly more decorative in appearance with the addition of moulded detail around the cross arm and the ornamentation of the foot with a few nicks and bevels. Decorative patterns in a variety of designs then begin to appear on the foot of the brooch. The knobs that are a distinguishing feature of the brooch change from being simple spherical or egg shapes to onion-shaped (from which comes the German name *Zwiebelknopffibeln* or 'onion-knobbed brooches'). Patterns along the length of the bow become popular: simple stamped repetitive designs such as crosses or arrows, which are sometimes left plain and sometimes filled with niello. Meanwhile, the form of the brooch is also changing; the bow section is becoming shorter and the foot longer and splayed at the end, giving far more pleasing proportions to the modern eye. Patterns

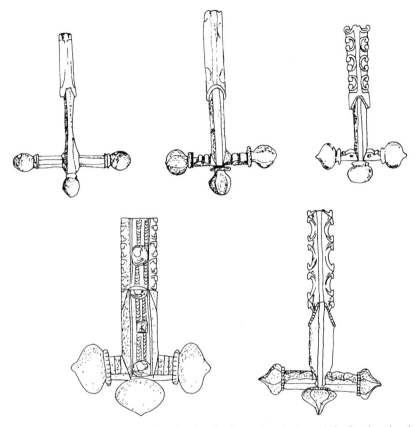

16. Typology of crossbow brooches showing the change in style through the fourth and early fifth centuries: (from left to right, top row) type 1, type 2, type 3/4; (bottom row) type 5, type 6. Originally the series contained type 3 and 4 brooches, established by Keller, but a later revision of the typology amalgamated the two types as they were not felt to be sufficiently dissimilar. (© Ellen Swift)

on the cross arm and foot become very standardised and predictable.

In the very late fourth century there is an innovation in the use of materials; instead of cast bronze or gilt bronze, brooches start to be made from sheet metal, which is cut and folded to form the hollow parts of the brooch. By now the crossbow brooch is almost unrecognisable, compared to very early examples. Some are very short and squat indeed, such as the example from Basel shown in figure 17, and are covered with niello decoration in very complex repeating patterns. These brooches often include medallions containing the Christian symbol, a chi-rho, or

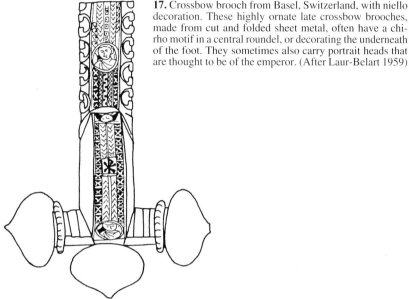

17. Crossbow brooch from Basel, Switzerland, with niello decoration. These highly ornate late crossbow brooches, made from cut and folded sheet metal, often have a chi-rho motif in a central roundel, or decorating the underneath of the foot. They sometimes also carry portrait heads that are thought to be of the emperor. (After Laur-Belart 1959)

portrait heads that are assumed to be of the emperor. They have moved well beyond any purely functional use and are covered in portentous symbols, reinforcing the power of the wearer through his association with the emperor and what is by now the state religion. Later in the fifth century they are found only in pure gold, with an openwork foot (a style of decoration popular in other jewellery types such as bracelets in this period).

Most object types undergo some changes like these through time, which enables us to give them an approximate date, though not all change as dramatically as the crossbow brooch. What is the significance of these changes? This is something that will be investigated in the final chapter.

4
Bracelets, finger-rings and earrings

Bracelets, rings and earrings sometimes share the same decorative style and motifs, with size being the only indicator of precise function. It has been suggested, though burial evidence is at present scarce, that such matching sets may have been worn together (Allason-Jones 1989: 24).

Bracelets

A wide variety of bracelets was worn in the Roman period. Bone and ivory examples do not survive well and jet, shale and glass are not as commonly found as copper alloy. Bracelets are known from the first century AD onwards, though they apparently became most popular in the fourth century AD and were especially favoured in *Pannonia*, the Roman province in modern-day Hungary, west of the Danube.

The two sources of information that we have on the way in which bracelets were worn in the Roman period are representations of people wearing dress accessories in Roman art (such as mummy portraits in Roman Egypt, one of the few media to show jewellery and dress accessories in any detail) and the position of bracelets in excavated graves (figure 18). These coincide to a fair degree in the evidence that they provide. Both suggest that across wide stretches of the Empire bracelets were commonly worn in pairs, with one bracelet on either wrist. There is evidence of variant practices in some areas of the Empire; for example in Hungary often as many as nine or ten bracelets were worn on the left wrist, with one or two on the right. It has been suggested by some archaeologists that in the later Empire it became common to wear larger numbers of bracelets generally and that this followed late antique fashion in which jewellery seems to have played an increased role.

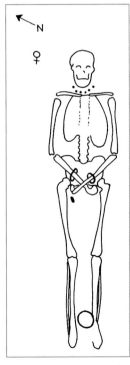

Glass, jet and shale, and bone bracelets

Glass bracelets are simple cast rings of glass, often coloured, and are rarely found complete.

18. A late Roman grave with bracelets worn at burial. The grave plan also shows a necklace around the neck and objects by the hand and foot. (After Burger 1966)

19. Copper alloy bracelet with hook and plate fastening. (© Corinium Museum, Cirencester)

They may have been more popular in antiquity than they appear as many could have been melted down and the glass recycled. They are not very often decorated. Shale or jet bracelets (without chemical analysis it is usually not possible to distinguish between these two materials) were made on a lathe by cutting away a central section from a flat disc. Again, they tend not to be decorated other than with engraved lines or bevels. Bone bracelets often consist of simple rings fastened together with copper alloy pins; some have a binding strip of copper alloy sheet wound around the joining section.

Copper alloy bracelets

These can be divided into numerous different types; just a few of the most popular are described below. Some are very plain, no more than a simple hoop of metal (figure 19). Some examples from northern Britain are shown in figure 20.

Snakeshead bracelets. The early examples of this type of bracelet in copper alloy are clearly imitations of gold and silver bracelets in the form of a snake, which were worn widely through the Empire in the early Roman period. They are not particularly common until the fourth century, and never so in Britain. One example that was found in Britain

20. Copper alloy bracelets. (© Tyne & Wear Museums)

21. Copper alloy bracelet with snakeshead terminals. (© Corinium Museum, Cirencester)

is shown in figure 21. In the Danube provinces of *Raetia* (south Germany), *Noricum* (Austria) and *Pannonia* (Hungary, west of the Danube), however, the type became extremely popular, with the proliferation of a wide variety of types and styles (figure 22). The bracelets are now characterised by two snake heads, one at either terminal, which may be extremely stylised (in some cases it takes quite a lot of imagination to pick out the animal's features). Occasionally another animal seems to have been the primary inspiration; for example, a particular type found in *Noricum* appears to be based on a lion head,

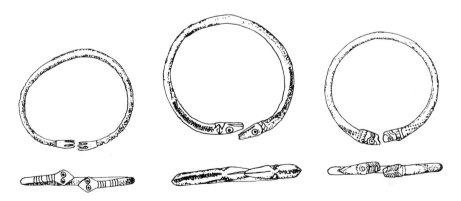

22. Copper alloy bracelets with snakeshead terminals from Bregenz, Austria. In the early Roman period, snakeshead bracelets were popular throughout the Roman world and were usually quite realistic, with visible scales and detailing of the head. By the late Roman period, in line with general trends in art, they are much more stylised and were particularly popular in the Danube region of the Roman Empire. (After Konrad 1997)

23. Imitation-cable copper alloy bracelet. These solid cast bracelets imitate those made from strands of wire twisted together. (© Corinium Museum, Cirencester)

with a muzzle and fur clearly visible.

Strip bracelets with punched decoration. An enormous variety of strip bracelets was produced in every part of the Western Empire and there is quite a substantial divergence in regional styles (Swift 2000a). Strip bracelets became particularly popular in the fourth century in many areas. Repeating patterns of motifs such as crosses, circles, flowers, chevrons and so on are the most common decoration. Notched zigzag patterns are popular in Britain, sometimes combined with circle and dot decoration.

Cable bracelets. A very popular bracelet type throughout the Roman Empire, cable jewellery, made from strands of wire twisted together, is also known in the pre-Roman period. Cable bracelets occur with two, three or four strands and are fastened with either a hook and eye or two hooks. There is some variation in the type of fastening preferred in different areas of the Empire; for example, cable bracelets from the Danube area tend to have the ends wrapped in a rolled sheet with two enclosing cuffs, surmounted by the hook and eye fastening (figure 1). These small differences enable us to look at the pattern of production in different areas of the Empire (Swift 2000a). Bracelets imitating cable bracelets made from solid cast metal are also known (figure 23).

Cog-wheel bracelets. This bracelet type is unique to Britain, save for a single example found at Oudenburg on the Channel coast (figure 24), and is idiosyncratic when compared to other types. Its distribution is

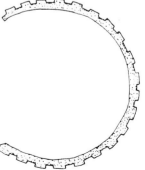

24. Cog-wheel bracelet from Oudenburg, Belgium; several bracelets from Britain were found in graves at this site on the Channel coast. (After Mertens and Van Impe 1971)

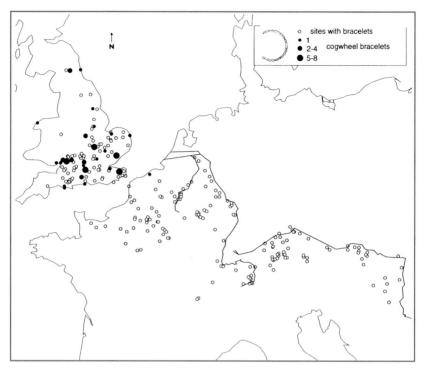

25. Map of the distribution of cog-wheel bracelets; it can be seen quite clearly that they are a British type. (© Ellen Swift)

shown in figure 25. It is made from a flat strip but instead of the strip being set flat against the wrist, as in most bracelet types, it is set edge-on so that there is a very narrow front face. The sides of the bracelet are cut out in a crenellated pattern and the final effect is very similar to a cog-wheel. Variations with grooves cut into the crenellations to give a toothed effect are also known.

Multiple-motif bracelets. This type of bracelet occurs both as a flat

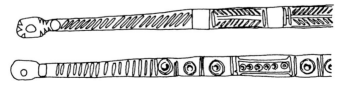

26. Multiple-motif bracelet. These bracelets are very characteristic of fourth-century assemblages and occur widely in Britain and more sporadically abroad. Many were found, for example, in a deposit at the temple site of Lydney in Gloucestershire, and as dress accessories placed in burials such as this example from Lankhills, Winchester, Hampshire. (After Griffiths in Clarke 1979)

strip bracelet and as a D-shaped cast bracelet. Both have hook and eye fastening and a complex pattern of symmetrical ornament (figure 26). Sometimes this repeats in alternate panels along the length of the bracelet; sometimes a central panel is flanked by two panels of identical decoration, one on either side. The panels of decoration often include zigzag and punched circle and dot patterns, hatched areas, diagonal notches and ribbing, rectangular motifs with dots in them, and so on. Multiple-motif bracelets were clearly made in Britain, as revealed by their distribution and extreme profusion in the province, but also reach northern France, Belgium and the Rhineland in small quantities. For example, a number have been found at the late Roman cemetery of Krefeld Gellep in the lower Rhine area.

Finger-rings

Finger-rings were common in the Roman period and were made from a variety of materials: gold, silver, glass, and copper alloy. Gold examples are often set with gemstones, sometimes with carved intaglios. The more prosaic materials, which we will concentrate on here as they are the types most likely to be found or seen in local museums, may also be decorated, for example with enamel or glass settings.

Introduced by the Romans and not worn in the pre-Roman period, rings seem to be fairly standardised throughout the Western Empire. For example, it is possible to use typologies constructed from French and German material to classify items found in Britain. This contrasts with the position of brooches, known before the conquest, which apparently have many regional variants both within one province and when one province is compared to another.

Finger-rings with a central setting

These are characteristic of the earlier Roman period. They usually have a D-sectioned hoop, lying flat against the finger but gently curving on the outer surface, and an oval bezel with a single central setting.

Jet and glass rings

An example of a jet ring is shown in figure 27. Jet and glass rings often mimic the forms found in other materials, for example rings with a central decorated bezel. Some glass rings are decorated with a spiralling trail of differently coloured glass.

27. Jet ring. (© Tyne & Wear Museums)

28. Snake ring. (© Corinium Museum, Cirencester)

Decorated copper alloy rings
Many such rings are simple hoops of wire, either flat or with a round section. Rings made from flat strips of metal often have punched or engraved decoration. Cast rings are also known, sometimes with a central flat bezel, with a motif such as a portrait head, engraved letters or perhaps a Christian symbol such as the chi-rho motif, or sometimes cast in the form of a snake, or with two snakeshead terminals. These are similar to snake bracelets and, like them, are more common in precious metals in the Roman period in Britain than in copper alloy, though a copper alloy example is shown in figure 28.

Ring-keys
This type of finger-ring, usually of copper alloy or sometimes of iron, could double as a functional key for a lock, presumably the lock on a small box or casket. One such example was found with fragments of the lock and casket itself at Elsenham, Essex. The rings have a projection with the key ward positioned so that it lies flat across the finger (figure 29). Some rings exist which clearly belong to the type but in which the projecting section is purely decorative rather than functional.

29. Ring-key, a type of dress accessory that combines ornament with a more functional role. The key would probably have been used to open a small box or casket. (© Corinium Museum, Cirencester)

Earrings
As a result of the work of Lindsay Allason-Jones (1989), earrings are now more readily recognised in the archaeological record than they once were. However, it is likely that many are still misclassified as fragments of wire. The main identifying feature of a copper alloy strand that was once an earring is its slightly pointed ends, or one pointed end. A variety of types exists, mostly simple hoops, decorated or undecorated, though 'drop' earrings with glass beads are also known, which mimic their more expensive counterparts in gold with precious stones. In the next chapter we turn to the subject of glass beads, which were used in the Roman period to make both earrings and bracelets.

5
Beads

Beads are common finds on archaeological sites in the Roman period. Roman beads are characteristically small geometric shapes of translucent glass, for example, cubes, spheres or hexagonal cylinders (see, for example, Guido 1978). These beads begin to appear in some quantities in the second and third centuries AD and are very common in the fourth century in particular, though perhaps this is because we have greater numbers of inhumation cemeteries for this century, a good source of beads, which were often included in graves.

The most popular beads in the late Roman period throughout the Western Empire are dark-blue diamond-faceted beads formed from a cube with the edges cut off, and long green hexagonal cylinder beads. In the very late Roman period some new types of beads began to appear that are more similar to those popular before the conquest and beyond the frontiers in the Roman period. These new beads are made of opaque rather than translucent glass and are often decorated with differently coloured trails. (See also the section on the glass-bead workshop at Trier in Chapter 2.) Most types of beads are quite widely found throughout the Western Empire (Swift 2000a). Beads also occur in other materials, such as bone and ivory, and, exceptionally, in semi-precious materials such as amber, coral and carnelian. It is thought that beads were used as amulets of some kind in the Roman period, particularly beyond the frontiers in Germany. Beads that carry representations of eyes or faces, or those that are in the shape of objects, are perhaps likely candidates for such a use.

Types of beads
A simple alphabetical glossary of some different types of Roman glass beads is given below. They are illustrated in figure 30.

Annular
In the Roman period, this type of bead is found only in very late Roman contexts dating to the end of the fourth century and the beginning of the fifth century. Late Roman annular beads are usually black with trails of coloured glass applied as decoration. These may be flattened into the surface of the bead when the trail is still molten or left as they are, in relief. A number of different patterns are commonly used: the bead may have coloured 'eyes', often using glass of more than one colour in concentric rings and circles; a simple wavy line may be applied, running around the circumference of the bead; a similar, but more

Annular	
Biconical	
Cylinder	
Diamond faceted	
Heart-shaped	
Hexagonal cylinder	
Melon	
Segmented	
Spherical	
Square cylinder	

30. Bead types commonly found in the Roman period.

angular, 'messy' line may be used, termed a 'scrabble'; or the bead may have a more complex pattern of eyes, with lines criss-crossing over and under each eye (a 'double swag'). Annular beads are known to have been produced in a glass workshop in Trier (see Chapter 2) but also occur very widely beyond the frontiers of the Roman Empire in both the early and late Roman periods (and, as already mentioned, are common in the pre- and post-Roman periods as well). They could therefore be said to represent a 'Germanic' and/or 'Celtic' style preference rather than a Roman one, though the question of who exactly wore these beads within the Roman Empire is a good deal more complex.

Biconical
This is a very common type, in the shape of two very squat, broadly based cones with the bases pressed together. Very small examples are

31. Yellow and blue bead strings composed of biconical beads, from Augst (inv. no. 1977.19555). (© Römerstadt Augusta Raurica, Switzerland/ Ursi Schild)

sometimes called 'lenticular'. They occur most frequently in blue, green and yellow. Long necklaces are often found that are made up entirely of hundreds of biconical beads (figure 31). Biconical beads with a more elongated shape are known but are not nearly so common.

Cylinder
This bead type is the easiest to produce, being simply made from pierced cylindrical rods of glass cut into different lengths. Cylinder beads may therefore be short disc-shaped beads, chunky beads as broad as they are long, or long cylinders.

Diamond-faceted
This type of bead occurs in fourth-century contexts within the Western Empire, often dating to the late fourth century. Diamond-faceted beads are very popular and widespread in this period. Although they are usually dark blue, green diamond-faceted beads are also known, and bone or carnelian beads of the same shape have been found in areas beyond the Roman frontiers. Similarly, glass diamond-faceted beads are also very widely found beyond the Roman frontiers and occur outside the Empire in earlier, second- and third-century contexts. They also continued to be worn in the post-Roman and early medieval periods in some areas of Europe, such as Hungary.

Gold-in-glass
These beads, colourless segmented sections of glass enclosing gold foil, are found widely in the Roman Empire from the first century onwards, though, with the exception of Britain, they did not reach the Western Empire until the fourth century. It is thought that they originated in the east, and trace-element analysis of the beads has shown that beads from Caerleon in Roman Wales and Faras in Roman Egypt exhibit close similarities (Boon 1977).

Heart-shaped

This type of bead appears to date to the later Roman period and is not common in Britain. Most examples come from Europe west of the Rhine. The bead is diamond-shaped in cross-section, with a central ridge parallel to the perforation. Heart-shaped beads are mostly found in blue and green glass.

Hexagonal cylinder

This type is similar to cylinder beads but made from a hexagonal rather than a cylindrical rod. It is useful to compare the colours and shapes of glass beads with necklaces of semi-precious stones. Necklaces of emeralds and gold chain are closely mimicked by counterparts in non-precious metals and glass. The emeralds are of a hexagonal cylinder shape, that of the naturally occurring crystal. Green glass beads in the same shape are some of the most popular found throughout the Empire and closely parallel the higher-status necklaces where they are found on a metal chain. These beads also occur in blue though they are less widespread in this colour.

Melon

This is an early Roman bead type, very distinctive and widely occurring (figure 32). Melon beads are usually made from turquoise glass or 'frit' – a substance with a vitreous glaze much like glass. Very occasionally they occur in other colours.

Segmented

These are one of the best-known types of Roman beads; they are

32. Melon beads, a very popular early Roman form. (© Tyne & Wear Museums)

made from lengths of cylindrical or spherical beads not quite detached from one another to give a segmented effect. The manufacture of this type is discussed in Chapter 2. They are known from the first century onwards. See also gold-in-glass beads.

Spherical

These are simple, small globular beads, very common in blue and green, though also found in a range of other colours.

Square cylinder

Another variant on the cylinder bead, this type is made from square-sectioned rods. These rods are sometimes cut to form perfectly square beads.

Sets of beads

From grave goods we can sometimes reconstruct the necklaces, bracelets or earrings on which the beads were threaded, though it should be borne in mind that so-called 'reconstructed' sets in museums may have been strung together without any knowledge of their precise arrangement or even that the beads necessarily belonged to the same necklace. Where an item was found in a grave around the neck of a skeleton, and where it has been carefully recorded, it is sometimes possible to try to reconstruct it more accurately (figure 33). Beads seem to have been female items in the Roman world and where they are found in grave contexts they are most often associated with female skeletons. Necklaces and bracelets were usually fastened with metal

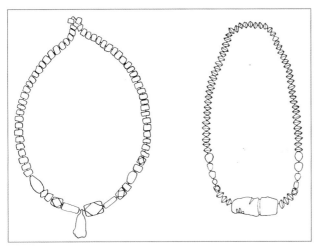

33. Necklaces of beads from Bregenz, Austria. (After Konrad 1997)

clasps and these often survive, giving some indication of the original positioning of the item. Sometimes beads were threaded on to wire to make particular kinds of earrings and bracelets. A good example is a bracelet type found in the Danube area that consists of strands of wire threaded with blue diamond-faceted and green hexagonal cylinder beads.

Colours

In the Roman period, glass beads appear to be most popular in blue and green, and they are also found in yellow, dark blue, white, colourless and black glass. Exceptionally, red may also be used. Opaque black and red are the most popular colours for late annular beads with trail decoration. Necklaces and bracelets from the cemetery at Bregenz, published in the 1990s, allow us to look at the way in which colours may have been combined with one another in necklaces, if the published arrangement can be taken to reproduce faithfully the original positioning of the beads in the grave. This seems quite likely, from comparisons with other carefully excavated examples, such as necklaces from Linz,

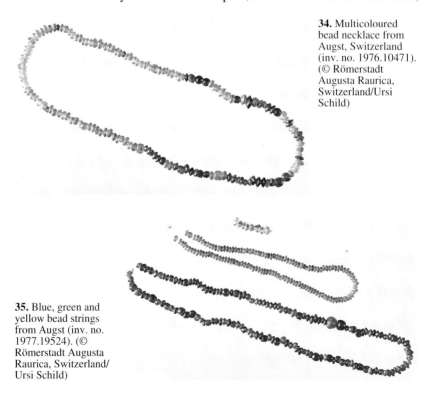

34. Multicoloured bead necklace from Augst, Switzerland (inv. no. 1976.10471). (© Römerstadt Augusta Raurica, Switzerland/Ursi Schild)

35. Blue, green and yellow bead strings from Augst (inv. no. 1977.19524). (© Römerstadt Augusta Raurica, Switzerland/ Ursi Schild)

nearby. At Bregenz, long strings of beads found as necklaces in graves are often composed of beads of two colours, apparently strung in an alternating pattern. Blue and green beads strung together to make a contrasting repeated design may have been a particularly popular combination. A central bead of a different colour or shape is frequently included, probably at the centre front of the necklace. Beads found at Augst have also been reconstructed as complete necklaces when discovered in grave contexts (figures 34 and 35).

Amber, carnelian and coral beads

These become rather more common in the late Roman period, though they are never widely found. They sometimes occur in graves with other unusual grave goods. For example, amber beads have been found in graves associated with Germanic-style brooches in very late fourth- and early fifth-century cemeteries that also contain male graves buried with weapons – an 'un-Roman' practice. Amber beads also seem to have a strong correlation with children's graves where they are found within the Roman Empire (Swift 2003).

Coral beads were found in the foreign graves at Lankhills, Winchester, which it is thought are of people who originated from Roman *Pannonia* or *Sarmatia* (modern-day Hungary). See Swift 2000a and 2000b for a detailed discussion of the evidence relating to these graves.

6
Pins

Pins made from copper alloy, bone and jet were widely used in the Roman period, and most museums with a Roman section have at least a small collection in their display cases. Glass pins are also known but are more unusual. There is a wide range of different types, based on the form and decoration of the head of the pin; the same type is often made in more than one raw material. Types can range from very simple, where the end is simply whittled down into a cone shape, to elaborate, for example a very detailed carved figure.

Techniques include both turning on a lathe and carving a blank to achieve the required shape. Those found most frequently on archaeological sites tend to be the more simple, as we might expect, and different types were popular at different times in the Roman period. Crummy (1983:19–20) points out that, while copper alloy and glass examples must have been manufactured in a workshop, bone pins could quite easily have been made by individuals, and cites worked bone and antler found in Colchester as evidence that they were produced there.

Commonly found pin types

Crummy (1983) classifies pins into a handful of commonly occurring types; these are listed below. Cool (1992) gives greater detail on more unusual types and provides a classification of twenty-seven groups for metal hairpins from southern Britain. Johns (1996) concentrates on elaborate pins with human busts or figures. Common pin types found at 9 Blake Street in York are illustrated in figure 36.

Conical head

This type of pin has a pointed cone-shaped head and occurs throughout the Roman period. They are often made of bone and many of these were perhaps made on the site where they were found.

Conical/rounded head with grooves, reels or bead-and-reel decoration

These can be divided into the more specific types, but the overall effect is very similar, with a combination of parallel grooves or reels and spherical or conical sections (figure 37). Sometimes the head is of a different material; for example a number of bone pins with disc-shaped jet heads were found at South Shields (Allason-Jones and Miket 1984: 78). Pins with simple grooves appear to be of earlier date than the more complex bead-and-reel variety, which are found commonly in fourth-century contexts.

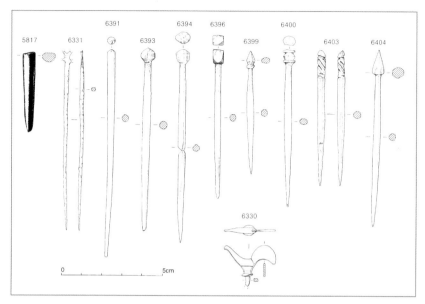

36. (Above) Pins from 9 Blake Street, York. (© York Archaeological Trust)

37. (Below) Bronze pin with bead-and-reel head. (© Corinium Museum, Cirencester)

Spherical head

This is another very simple type with a rounded head, which may be inclined towards the elliptical, lenticular or 'onion-shaped', or may be a true sphere. This type of pin was popular from the second century onwards.

Faceted head

Many pins with faceted heads are very similar to late Roman diamond-faceted beads, as discussed in Chapter 5. They are cube-shaped, with the edge taken off each corner to form a diamond-shaped face on each side of the cube. Crummy (1983: 23) comments that bone examples appear to have presented a considerable technical challenge to the manufacturer, who rarely achieved a perfect shape. Jet examples appear to be more successful. This pin type is found from the mid to late third century onwards.

Anthropomorphic head

These often depict a female figure, either just the bust or a complete figurine. Some can be identified with particular goddesses such as Venus (Johns 1996). Examples in bone and copper alloy are probably copying higher-status decorative pins of gold and silver. Some even show the type of elaborate, piled-up hairstyle popular in the earlier Roman period, which would have necessitated the use of many pins to hold the hair in place.

Hairstyles

Pins were mostly used in women's hair, though it is speculated that they could also have been used as clothes fasteners. They have been found in inhumation burials close to the head, for example at the Butt Road cemeteries in Colchester (Crummy 1983: 19). Cool's extensive study of pins in Roman Britain shows that they were made of an appropriate length for the type of hairstyle fashionable at the time. In the early Roman period, the preferred hairstyle was for hair piled up on top of the head, requiring long pins to hold it in place. In the later Roman period hairstyles were flatter on the head, and from grave contexts, where pins are usually found beneath the skull, they seem to have been used to pin the hair at the back of the head rather than on top of the head. The length of pins shows a corresponding decline (Cool 1992: 174). This change in length is very consistent across all pin types in Roman Britain. It can be surmised from this that the same fashions prevailed throughout the province, though there is some variation in the types of hairpins themselves.

Regional pin types

Cool shows that pin types in Britain exhibit considerable regional variation, with three main areas of distribution in the early Roman period (Cool 1992). Groups of pins with the same decorative patterns cluster together in three roughly overlapping areas: one with a fairly large distribution in a diagonal line running from East Anglia to the south-west; one in northern Kent and the London area; and one in the west around Gloucestershire and Somerset. In the late Roman period, however, these distinctions seem to disappear and the same pin types are favoured throughout the province. Cool also finds some pin types with an exclusive distribution on military sites, which raises some interesting questions about who was wearing these objects: presumably not the soldiers themselves, as they probably did not have long tresses that needed pinning up; perhaps, then, women who travelled with the army. The best-known military dress accessory worn by soldiers is the belt set, the subject of the next chapter.

7
Belt sets

The use of buckles and belt fittings seems to have been primarily among the Roman army, and the waist-belt had become an established part of soldiers' dress by the middle of the first century AD. A simple belt set might consist of a buckle attached to a flat plate, which would be fixed to the leather of the belt strap, and a tag or 'strap-end' attached to the other end of the strap to prevent wear on the leather itself. The most complicated Roman belt sets consist of many different plates and attachments: flat strips of metal to strengthen the belt along its length, and loops or rings that could be used to fasten other items to the belt. Occasionally a complete belt set is found *in situ* in a grave, and in this way the appearance of the full set can be reconstructed. Often, though, the component parts of the set are found in single pieces. Where we have evidence from inhumation burials (more common in the late Roman period), belts were not often worn at burial but were more likely to be placed at the feet of a corpse. In the earlier Roman period, there are fewer cemeteries with inhumation burials (as opposed to cremation burials) so we do not have good evidence of whether belts were worn at burial or not.

Belt sets are most frequently found at military sites in the early Roman empire and in the first part of the fourth century. In the later fourth century and the fifth century, when Roman-style belt sets were still produced (despite the fact that the Roman authorities were no longer in control in some areas, including Britain), they seem to occur frequently on civilian sites as well. However, we know less about settlement patterns in this period, and the context of many finds is no longer known.

Decorative style

Roman belt sets are often decorated, the flat surface of the plate providing an ideal field for ornament, and several characteristic styles of engraving, casting and inlay were used. Buckle loops of various shapes were used; typically, annular for third century buckles, with the D-shaped buckle the dominant type in the late Roman period. Regional variants are known in the shape of the buckle, for example rectangular buckles from *Pannonia* and further east.

Enamel

This was a popular decorative technique used to adorn buckles in the second and third centuries. Enamelled buckle plates are widely found in the Roman Empire and several have been discovered in Britain on

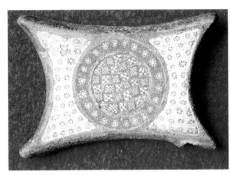

38. Enamelled belt plate from York with multicoloured millefiori enamel. (© York Archaeological Trust)

military sites such as the forts at Leicester, and at York (figure 38). This example has a complex millefiori pattern made up of many tiny segments of coloured enamel. The central roundel can be paralleled by designs on circular studs from Richborough, South Shields and Caerleon (Cool, Lloyd-Morgan and Hooley 1995: 1535).

Zoomorphic ornament

The buckle loop of late Roman buckles was often decorated in a style known as 'zoomorphic' (figures 39–40). This means that the decoration resembles animals, though these are often very stylised, and it is

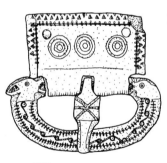

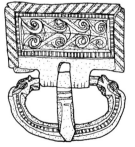

sometimes difficult to work out which particular animal is being represented. The style of decoration is very different from earlier Roman representations of animals in art, and, because of this and because it is similar to early medieval metalwork styles, late Roman belt sets were initially thought to be Germanic in origin – either coming from Germany itself with members of Germanic tribes who fought in the Roman army, or influenced by Germanic styles popular in the late Roman Empire. Fuel was added to the flames with the discovery

39. Buckles with zoomorphic ornament. It is difficult to distinguish exactly what animals are represented, as the buckles are very stylised, and for many years they were thought not to be of Roman origin at all but inspired by Germanic metalwork. It is now recognised that many follow common Roman themes, depicting animals such as dolphins, for example, which are widely portrayed on Roman mosaics. (After Sommer 1984)

40. Buckle with zoomorphic terminals from grave 1, Dorchester-on-Thames, Oxfordshire. (© Ashmolean Museum, Oxford)

of some of these belt sets in the Germanic homelands far beyond the Roman frontier. It has since been accepted, however, that the animal ornament is just part of the general tendency towards more stylised, less representational art in the late Roman world.

The choice of animals can be sourced to Roman prototypes. For example, one of the most popular motifs is a dolphin, which was often used in Roman decoration. Two animals are often confronted on the loop, either facing away from each other, biting the conjunction with the plate, or facing towards each other at the centre front of the loop. The most frequently occurring shape for the loop is a D-shape, with the belt plate attached to the flat side.

Chip-carving

Very elaborate chip-carved belt sets with a wealth of ornament are a widespread and well-known feature of late antique culture. They were not much worn in Britain but are found in other provinces, particularly along the Roman frontier in Germany on the Rhine and the Danube. The decoration covers the whole surface of a number of plates that are attached to the belt. Geometric designs intertwine with leaf and tendril motifs in a repeating pattern. 'Chip-carved' refers to the technique of production and the carving of the original wooden moulds. The belts that we see now are the dull greenish or brownish colour of bronze whose surface has been corroded by exposure to air and moisture, but when they were made they would have been a bright brassy colour, and the numerous faceted surfaces in the decoration must have caught and reflected the light, making these belt sets very showy items of dress. Perhaps they were polished to keep them bright, though we must guard against taking analogies from the modern military too far. As might be expected, these belt sets were worn by those in the upper ranks of the

41. Buckle plate with niello decoration. Niello was a very popular decorative technique in the late Roman period. The design would be engraved into the surface and the engraving inlaid with a black paste of metal sulphide, which would stand out against the bright surface of the metal. (After Mertens and Van Impe 1971)

Roman army, and we have some documented evidence that they were used as insignia of office in the late Empire.

Niello

Some smaller belt plates were also highly decorated, using a method very popular in late antiquity – that of including a different coloured inlay to contrast with the bright surface of the metal. Niello inlay was used in both the early and the late Roman periods, particularly on belt plates of precious metal, or those that had been tinned or gilded. A silver or gold surface would be engraved with a pattern; sometimes a figurative representation, of a person, perhaps a god or goddess, or a scene from mythology. Sometimes animals would also be used; see, for example, figure 41, a belt set from Oudenburg. The pattern would be emphasised by filling in the engraved lines with a black metal sulphide inlay.

Openwork

Some openwork examples are shown in figures 42 and 43. Again, openwork decoration was used in both the earlier and later Roman

42. (Left) Buckle with openwork decoration found at Amiens, France. (© Ashmolean Museum, Oxford)

43. (Below) Buckle plate with openwork decoration. (After Mertens and Van Impe 1971)

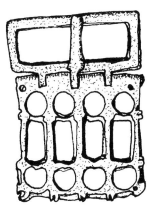

periods, with some differences in the detail of the ornamentation. In the Antonine period openwork designs were particularly popular, and often consisted of quite elaborate patterns. Fourth- and fifth-century openwork belt sets have cut-outs of round, rectangular or other geometric shapes, characteristically including a motif that looks to modern eyes very much like a keyhole (figure 43).

Engraving and punched work

Belt sets not sporting the above techniques could still be finely decorated. The whole surface of the belt plate might be covered with a fine web of engraved lines, in grids, or with overlapping concentric circles or rows of leaf-shapes and triangles. In this way the belt sets perhaps mimicked the busy surface of the chip-carved sets. Simpler decoration, punched circles and dots, squares and triangles, were also used.

Belt sets are one of the few object types that continued to be produced and worn well into the fifth century, for example the double horse-head

44. Double horse-head buckle from grave 2, Dorchester-on-Thames, Oxfordshire. These buckles are thought to have a date range that extends into the early fifth century. (© Ashmolean Museum, Oxford)

45. Strap-end from Bifrons. The animal decoration is in a style known as the 'Quoit brooch style', thought to be an indigenous development in the early fifth century. (© Maidstone Museum and Art Gallery)

46. Strap-end from Winterbourne Gunner, Wiltshire (inv. no. KAS 1954.620.c). (© Salisbury and South Wiltshire Museum)

buckles (figure 44) found principally in the south-west of England, which sometimes occur in Anglo-Saxon graves. Some strap-ends that are thought to be of early fifth-century date are shown in figures 45 and 46. The animals that decorate them continued to be a popular motif in the early medieval period, though the style in which they are portrayed developed considerably and the animals become more and more difficult to recognise. New Anglo-Saxon and Frankish types eventually replaced the Roman styles that lingered in the south-west of Britain and in northern Gaul.

8
Interpreting dress accessories

In the previous chapters, an overview of common types of dress accessories in the Roman period has been provided. After the identification and cataloguing of finds from archaeological sites and museum collections, however, what happens next? How can we use objects such as dress accessories to study the Roman world?

Production and trade

As mentioned in Chapter 2, the distribution of objects may be revealing about trade networks and production systems in antiquity. We may contrast the widespread distribution of crossbow brooches, the most popular types of which were produced in a centralised military factory, with the small regional distributions of various types of dress accessory that were obviously produced in only one workshop and traded in its immediate environs. Similarly, the widespread distribution of elaborate chip-carved belt sets along the Rhine and Danube frontiers may be contrasted with the later proliferation of regional types of belt sets in northern Gaul and Britain (Sommer 1984, Swift 2000a).

The restricted distribution patterns of many types of dress accessories in common, inexpensive materials such as glass and copper alloy can be contrasted with those of some high-status dress accessories in precious metals, which had a much wider distribution. They appealed to the taste of the élite, which was more uniform throughout the provinces, and also the transport of valuable goods offered a better return on the costs of long-distance trade. The production and distribution of objects, however, has to be considered in relation to the demand for the object, which raises questions of identity, fashion and culture.

Clothing and fashion

The most immediately obvious use to the archaeologist for dress accessories is to reconstruct the dress and clothing fashions of different periods in antiquity, and this has been touched on briefly in previous chapters. In the early Roman Empire, rings and brooches are more popular; in the late Roman Empire, bracelets and necklaces become the preferred items of dress. Trends like these, which vary through time, are often described as 'fashion'. They can of course be exhibited in a wide variety of goods – there are fashions in food, for example, or in cars, or houses – but the most immediate association of the term 'fashion' is with clothing and appearance, which is interesting in itself. In a post-industrial society, changes in styles of dress have accelerated at an astonishing rate, so that we are currently used to talking in terms of decades rather than centuries. We link changes in dress to wider changes in society and culture; for example, the Arts and Crafts movement of the late nineteenth and early twentieth century is associated with dress, styles of jewellery, furnishings and fabrics, paintings, and a particular social and political outlook. In antiquity, and particularly in prehistory, change was much slower, and styles of dress are often more associated with regional groups who did not change their dress customs for centuries at a time. In the Roman period, however, social organisation was on a scale more similar to the one that we recognise today, and we can see fashion operating in the Roman world in a similar manner to today's changes in style, though dress styles apparently change over longer time spans of perhaps a hundred rather than ten years. Though we may recognise that these changes in dress style (for example, rings becoming less popular through time and bracelets becoming more popular) are indicative of wider social and cultural change, we cannot reconstruct exactly the cultural, social and political transformations that are related to these changes through an examination of dress alone.

Dress and identity
Provincial Roman dress

We can turn to the archaeological record to examine the universal adoption of Roman-style culture in the provinces. By the mid second century AD, Roman-style dress appears to have been well established all over the Empire. The same types of dress accessory are widely worn and we can see from examples such as the second-century Snettisham hoard (Johns 1997) that rings and bracelets with the same decorative style were being produced in several different areas of the Empire. Until this find was made, it was commonly assumed that some types of jewellery and dress accessories of high quality must have been made in Rome and exported to Britain, but the jeweller's scrap and tools and objects of the Snettisham hoard proved that they could also have come from a workshop in the province itself.

From studies of people represented on tombstones in the Western provinces, it has been established that the same dress customs prevailed across Western Europe (always supposing that this is representative) by the late Roman period. This was not the wearing of a toga, which remained an élite garment and eventually became a purely ceremonial item of dress (Stone 1994), but for men a combination of a hooded tunic and leggings, rather similar to our stereotypical image of a medieval peasant, and for women a rather longer tunic (Wilde 1985). Similarly, fashions in dress accessories were fairly uniform. Some types of dress accessory, such as the beads that made up necklaces and bracelets, conformed more to Empire-wide fashions than others. These general trends may not have been a conscious attempt by wearers to become 'Roman' or even 'provincial Roman', but they are indicative of the way in which Roman-inspired culture became ubiquitous in the Western Empire.

Regional variation in dress

In *Pannonia* (modern-day Hungary west of the Rhine), a particular dress custom at burial is known from the fourth century. In cemeteries across the area, women were buried with bracelets placed on the left arm, and in some cemeteries young women have very many of these bracelets, ten or more, while older women only have a couple. This dress custom at burial is not known from anywhere else within the Empire (or indeed outside it) and was one of the factors leading to the identification of some travellers from a different part of the Empire at the Lankhills cemetery in Winchester (Clarke 1979, Swift 2000b: 69–75). In this particular example, it seems to be the case that people were using dress accessories as a means of constructing or representing their dead in a particular way, with a specific identity.

Gender

Dress is used as a means of accentuating the differences between male and female, and numerous examples could be cited, from prehistory to the present day. Archaeologists and those in the field of cultural studies often discuss the idea of gender separately from the concept of biological sex. Biological sex is a given, but gender can be constructed through the use of items of dress and accessories that are particularly associated with male or female identity. Dress accessories therefore have an important role to play in the construction of gendered identities. In the Roman period, some items such as rings and brooches were worn by both sexes, while bracelets, necklaces and earrings were invariably worn by women. Very late and post-Roman cemeteries are interesting because in some cases we can see a different use of dress accessories at burial, in which earrings and bracelets may instead be items of male dress. These graves have sometimes been associated with the barbarians who fought both within the Roman army and on the opposing side during the breakdown of the Western Roman Empire. Whether they are the graves of barbarians or not, they certainly show a divergence in the use of dress accessories to construct a particular gendered identity.

Dress accessories as symbols

In a historical period such as the Roman period, additional information is sometimes available that enables us to examine the use and significance of particular items of dress beyond their association with a particular gender or culture. If we examine references to jewellery and dress accessories in literary and historical sources, there are some interesting examples. Perhaps the most famous Roman 'dress accessory' is the laurel wreath worn by the emperor. In the early Roman period, there was a complex system of laurel wreaths awarded to people who had achieved various kinds of military triumph. There are numerous references by authors such as Suetonius alluding to these and other symbolic items of dress in Roman society. The iron ring worn by the Equestrian order is another early Roman example. Inevitably, though, these sources refer to very specific periods, places and items, and there is a limit to how far we can use them to interpret the use and symbolism of dress accessories in general in the wider Empire, especially since they usually refer to élite culture.

In the later Roman period, certain dress accessories, such as the belt set and some types of brooch, became particularly associated with the Roman military. The use of some types of bow brooch such as the P-brooch seems to have originated in the Danube provinces of the Roman Empire, a heavily militarised region. It is thought that P-brooches developed into crossbow brooches, which were also most common at first in the Danube provinces, and these became widespread in the fourth century as symbols of the military and of high-status civilians. The most widespread and frequently occurring type, made from cast copper alloy with onion-shaped terminals and a distinctive arrangement of circle and dot motifs on the foot of the brooch, is thought to have been produced in a military production centre in *Pannonia*, the Roman province occupying part of modern-day Hungary, though other less common types were probably produced in more localised workshops (Swift 2000b: 48).

Bishop and Coulston (1993) provide a useful summary of military belt fittings in their book on Roman military equipment. In the first century, two belts were commonly worn, one to hold the dagger and one for the sword, but during the course of the century it became more usual for just one belt to be worn. With the belt set's intimate association with the sword (the most obvious signifier of military identity) it too became associated with military identity. Soldiers depicted on tombstones are often shown with their belt around their waist, and the various fittings and fastenings attached to the belt are sometimes clearly visible. In the late Roman period, wide military belt sets are worn by both the military and high-status civilian officials, and the *Notitia Dignitatum*, an official administrative document dating to the beginning of the fifth century AD, depicts them among items produced by military factories in this period.

From this discussion, it is therefore evident that dress accessories had many roles beyond the purely decorative. Once they are identified and catalogued, dress accessories can be used to investigate many different facets of the Roman world. This book is merely a starting point; those interested in the subject can pursue it in many other scholarly books, some of which are listed in the next chapter.

9
Further reading

Allason-Jones, L. 'Earrings in Roman Britain', *British Archaeological Reports*, 1989.

Allason-Jones, L., and Miket, R. *Catalogue of Small Finds from South Shields Roman Fort*. Society of Antiquaries of Newcastle upon Tyne, 1984.

Bishop, M. C., and Coulston, J. C. *Roman Military Equipment from the Punic Wars to the Fall of Rome*. Batsford, 1993.

Boon, G. 'Gold-in-glass beads from the ancient world', *Britannia*, 8 (1977), 193–207.

Clarke, G. 'The Roman cemetery at Lankhills', *Winchester Studies*, 3 (1979), Clarendon Press.

Cool, H. 'Roman metal hair-pins from southern Britain', *The Archaeological Journal*, 147 (1992), 148–82.

Cool, H., Lloyd-Morgan, G., and Hooley, A. *Finds from the Fortress. The Archaeology of York*, volume 17, Council for British Archaeology (for York Archaeological Trust), 1995.

Crummy, N. *The Roman Small Finds from Excavations in Colchester*. Colchester Archaeological Reports, 2 (1983), Colchester Archaeological Trust.

Garbsch, J. *Die norisch-pannonische Frauentracht im 1 und 2 Jarhhundert*. Münchner Beiträge zur vor und Frügeschichte, 11 (1965), C. H. Beck, München.

Guido, M. 'Glass beads of the prehistoric and Roman periods in Britain and Ireland', *Society of Antiquaries Research Report*, 35 (1978), Society of Antiquaries.

Hattatt, R. *Ancient and Romano-British Brooches*. Dorset Publishing Company, 1982.

Hattatt, R. *Iron-Age and Roman Brooches*. Oxbow Books, 1985.

Hattatt, R. *Brooches of Antiquity: A Third Selection from the Author's Collection*. Oxbow Books, 1987.

Johns, C. *The Jewellery of Roman Britain*. UCL Press, 1996.

Johns, C. *The Snettisham Roman Jeweller's Hoard*. The British Museum, 1997.

Keller, E. *Die spätrömischen Grabfunde in Südbayern*. C. H. Beck, Munich, 1971.

Snape, M. 'Roman Brooches from North Britain', *British Archaeological Reports*, 235 (1993).

Sommer, M. 'Die Gurtel und Gurtelbeschlage des 4 und 5 Jahrhunderts im Romischen Reich', *Bonner Hefte zur Vorgeschichte*, 22 (1984), Bonn.

Stone, S. 'The toga: from national to ceremonial costume' in *The World of Roman Costume*, edited by J. Sebasta and L. Bonfante. University of Wisconsin Press, 1994.

Swift, E. 'Regionality in dress accessories in the late Roman West', *Monographies Instrumentum*, 11 (2000a), editions Monique Mergoil, Montagnac.

Swift, E. *The End of the Western Roman Empire: An Archaeological Investigation*. Tempus, 2000b.

Swift, E. 'Transformations in meaning: amber and glass beads across the Roman frontier', pages 48–57 in G. Carr, E. Swift and J. Weekes (editors), *TRAC 2002: Proceedings of the Twelfth Annual Theoretical Roman Archaeology Conference, Canterbury 2002*. Oxbow Books, 2003.

Van der Sleen, W. *A Handbook on Beads*. Halbart, Liège, 1973.

Wilde, J. 'The clothing of Britannia, Gallia Belgica and Germania Inferior', *Aufsteig und Niedergange der Romischen Welt*, II 12.3 (1985), 362–422.

10
Museums

Arbeia Roman Fort and Museum, Baring Street, South Shields NE33 2BB. Telephone: 0191 456 1369. Website: www.twmuseums.org.uk/arbeia

The British Museum, Great Russell Street, London WC1B 3DG. Telephone: 020 7323 8299. Website: www.thebritishmuseum.ac.uk

Corinium Museum, Park Street, Cirencester, Gloucestershire GL7 2BX. Telephone: 01285 655611. Website: www.cotswold.gov.uk/museum (Closed for redevelopment until spring 2004.)

Hull and East Riding Museum, High Street, Hull HU1 1PS. Telephone: 01482 613902. Website: www.hullcc.gov.uk/museums

Museum of Antiquities, University of Newcastle upon Tyne, Newcastle upon Tyne NE1 7RU. Telephone: 0191 222 7846 or 0191 222 7849. Website: http://museums.ncl.ac.uk

Museum of London, London Wall, London EC2Y 5HN. Telephone: 020 7600 3699. Website: www.museum-london.org.uk

The Roman Museum, Longmarket, Butchery Lane, Canterbury, Kent. Telephone: 01227 785575. Website: www.canterbury.gov.uk

Verulamium Museum, St Michaels, St Albans, Hertfordshire AL3 4SW. Telephone: 01754 768837. Website: www.verulamium.com

Index